THE HUMAN BODY

SEYMOUR SIMON

Smithsonian | Collins

An Imprint of HarperCollinsPublishers

Special thanks to Don E. Wilson, Senior Scientist, National Museum of Natural History, Smithsonian Institution, for his invaluable contribution to this book.

PHOTO AND ART CREDITS: page 3: John M. Daugherty/Photo Researchers, Inc.; page 4: Alfred Pasieka/Photo Researchers, Inc.; page 5: Simon Fraser/Photo Researchers, Inc.; page 7: SPL/Photo Researchers, Inc.; pages 8-9: Don Farrall/Getty Images; page 10: Susumu Nishinaga/Photo Researchers, Inc.; page 11: Eye of Science/Photo Researchers, Inc.; page 12: Steve Gschmeissner/Photo Researchers, Inc.; page 14: © Ralph Hutchings/Visuals Unlimited; page 15: Prof. P. M. Motta/Univ. "La Sapienza," Rome/Photo Researchers, Inc.; page 16: SPL/Photo Researchers, Inc.; page 19: © Nucleus Medical Art/Visuals Unlimited; page 20: Steve Gschmeissner/Photo Researchers, Inc.; page 23: Howard Sochurek/Medical Images; page 25: Art by Ann Neumann; page 26: David M. Phillips/Visuals Unlimited; page 28: © Dr. Fred Hossler/Visuals Unlimited; page 29: Innerspace Imaging/Photo Researchers, Inc.; page 30: Véronique Estiot/Photo Researchers, Inc.; page 33: Vero/Carlo/Photo Researchers, Inc.; page 34: Susan Leavines/Photo Researchers, Inc.; page 37: Prof. P. M. Motta/Univ. "La Sapienza," Rome/Science Photo Library; page 38: © Lester Lefkowitz/CORBIS; pages 40, 41: SPL/Photo Researchers, Inc.; page 43: James Cavallini/Photo Researchers, Inc.; page 44: Christian Darkin/Photo Researchers, Inc.; page 46: Eye of Science/Photo Researchers, Inc.; page 47: David M. Phillips/Photo Researchers, Inc.; page 48: Biophoto Associates/Photo Researchers, Inc.; page 50: hybrid medical animation/Photo Researchers, Inc.; page 51: James Cavallini/Photo Researchers, Inc.; page 52: Bill Longcore/Photo Researchers, Inc.; page 53: Mehau Kulyk/Photo Researchers, Inc.; page 54: John Bavosi/Photo Researchers, Inc.; page 57: Susumu Nishinaga/Photo Researchers, Inc.; page 58: Art by Ann Neumann; page 61: SPL/Photo Researchers, Inc.

The Human Body
Copyright © 2008 by Seymour Simon
Manufactured in China.

Library of Congress Cataloging-in-Publication Data
Simon, Seymour.
  The human body / Seymour Simon. — 1st ed.
    p.   cm.
  ISBN 978-0-06-055541-2 (trade bdg.) — ISBN 978-0-06-055542-9 (lib bdg.)
  1. Body, human—Juvenile literature. 2. Human physiology—Juvenile literature. I. Title.
QP37.S55 2008   2007033300
612—dc22   CIP
                                                                                          AC

1 2 3 4 5 6 7 8 9 10
❖
First Edition

Smithsonian Mission Statement

For more than 160 years, the Smithsonian has remained true to its mission, "the increase and diffusion of knowledge." Today the Smithsonian is not only the world's largest provider of museum experiences supported by authoritative scholarship in science, history, and the arts but also an international leader in scientific research and exploration. The Smithsonian offers the world a picture of America, and America a picture of the world.

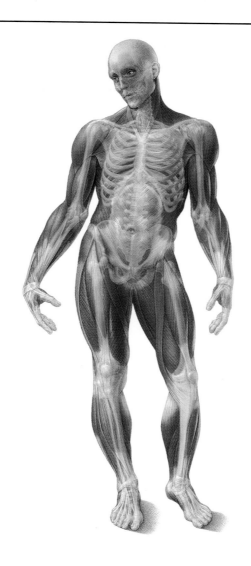

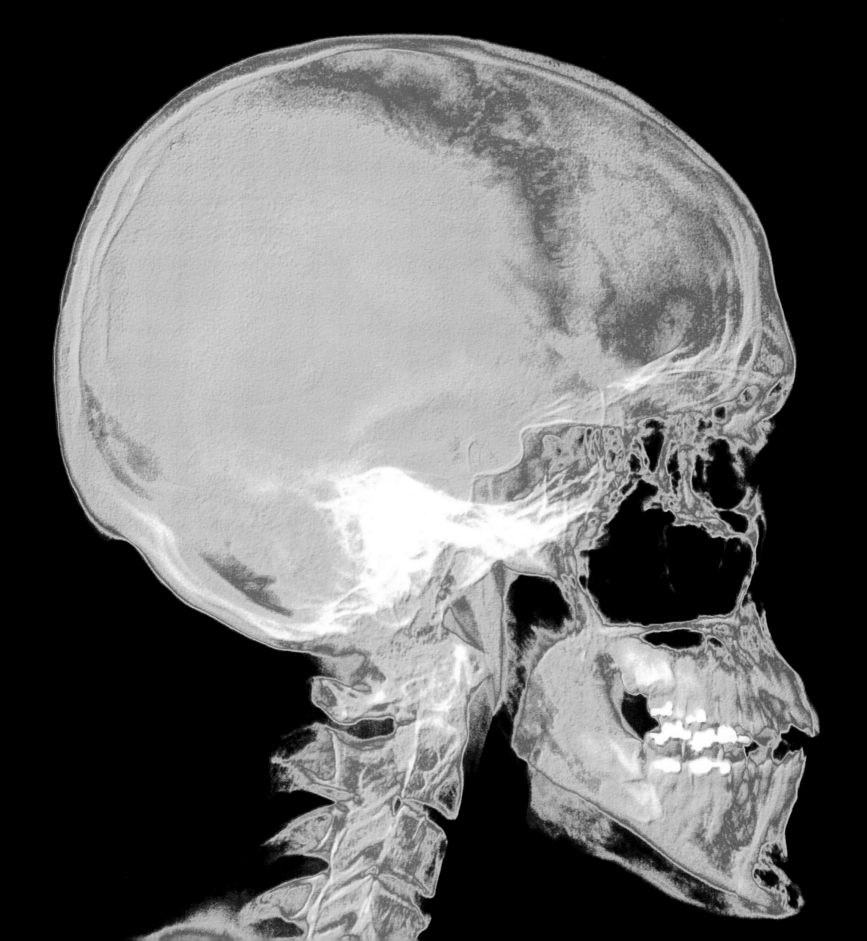

From early times, people have looked and marveled at muscles and bones, the heart and the stomach, the ears and the eyes, and the other body parts they could examine. But not until the discovery of **X-rays** in the nineteenth century were doctors and scientists able to see inside a body without cutting it open.

By the second half of the twentieth century, computerized imaging instruments were able to show the living body in action. Nowadays we can picture and explore the workings of microscopic cells and the largest systems that make up the amazing machine we call the human body.

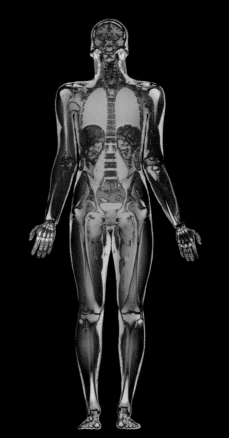

The tiniest living blocks of the body are **cells**. They are so small that you can't see them with your unaided eye. Cells were first discovered about four hundred years ago when the microscope was invented. Your body has about 100 trillion cells. That's 100 followed by twelve zeros! (No one has counted them all, so it's just a good guess. If you were to count one cell a second nonstop, you would need millions of years to count a single trillion cells!)

There are about 200 different kinds of cells in the human body. Each kind of cell has a different size, shape, and function in the body. But most cells are alike in that they have a membrane that surrounds and protects them, a central control center, called a nucleus, and a jellylike material, called cytoplasm, that fills the cell.

Cells divide and multiply. That allows the body to grow and to replace damaged or worn cells. Some cells, such as white blood cells, live for just a few days, while others, such as nerve cells, can live for years.

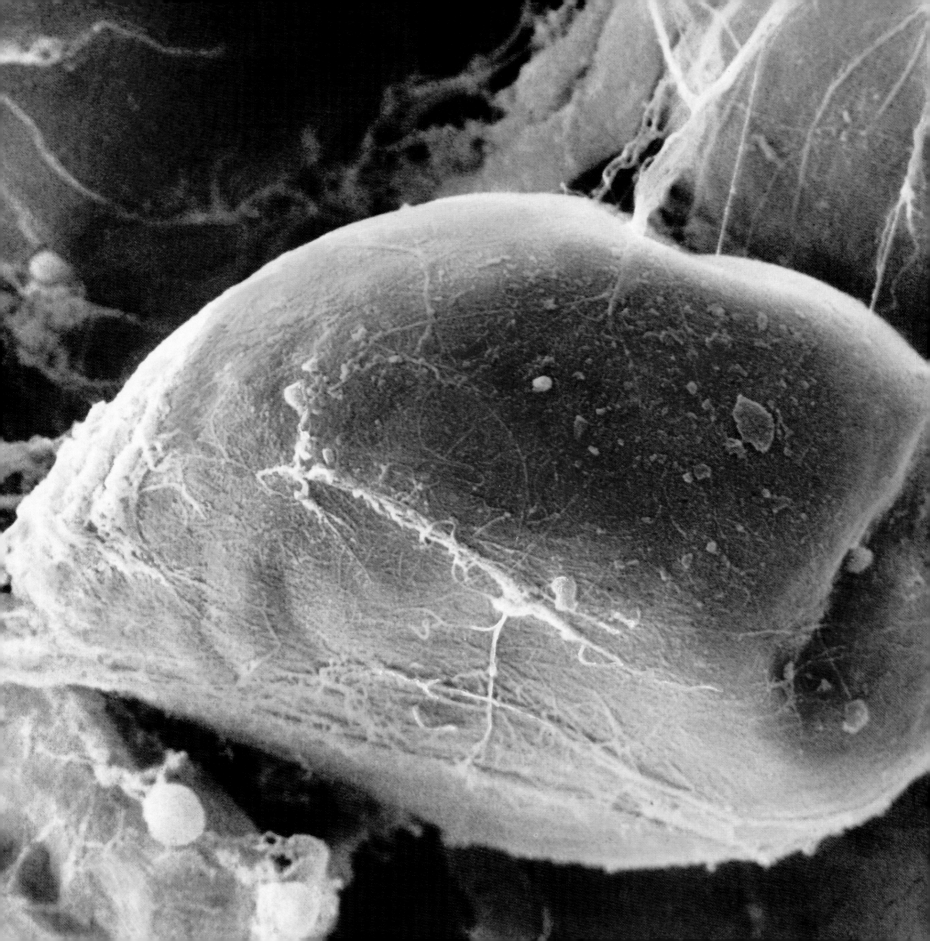

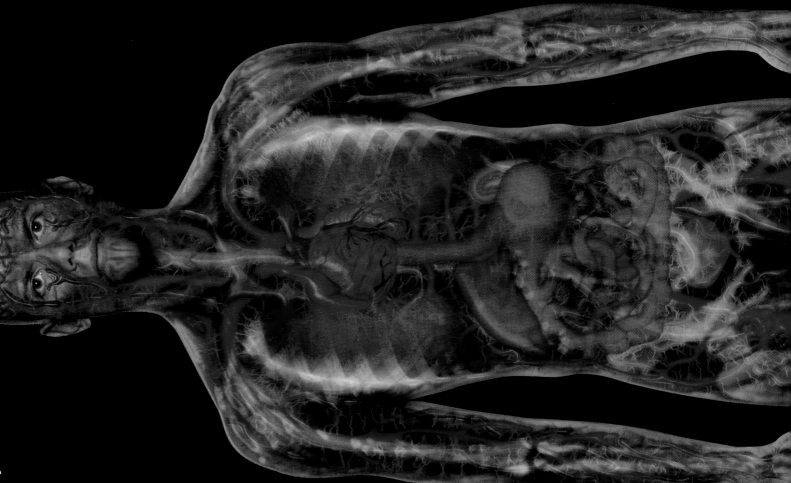

Here are the twelve major systems that make up the human body:

THE INTEGUMENTARY SYSTEM
is the outer covering of the body. It's made up of skin, hair, and nails.

THE SKELETAL SYSTEM
is the body's framework of bones, **cartilage**, and ligaments.

THE MUSCULAR SYSTEM
works together with the skeletal system to allow you to move.

THE CIRCULATORY SYSTEM
controls circulation, the flow of blood around the body.

THE RESPIRATORY SYSTEM
supplies the body with oxygen, a gas people need to live.

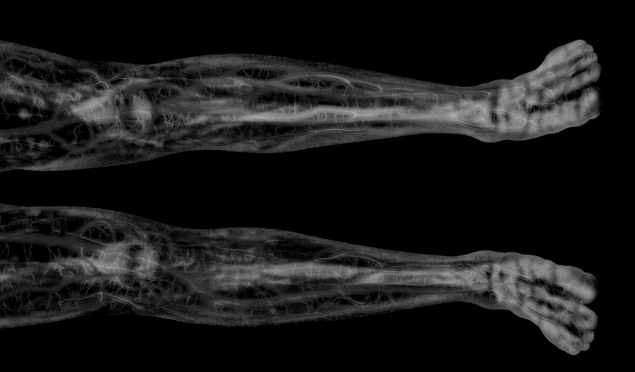

takes in food and breaks it down
into the fuel that the body needs.

THE NERVOUS SYSTEM
is the body's control system.

THE URINARY AND
EXCRETORY SYSTEMS
get rid of the body's wastes.

THE IMMUNE AND
LYMPHATIC SYSTEMS
help protect the body from infections.

THE REPRODUCTIVE SYSTEM
works so that a man and a woman
together can have children.

Cells, **tissues, and organs** working together make up twelve body systems. Like the players on a team, each of the systems relies on all the others to keep the body healthy and functioning.

Skin, along with hair and nails, is the boundary between your insides and the world outside. Skin forms a protective covering that keeps out water and germs and filters out harmful rays of sunlight. Skin helps the body to maintain a constant temperature no matter how warm or cold it is outside. Skin is not flat and smooth. The patterns of skin whorls on your fingers are called fingerprints. Every person in the world has his or her own distinctive set of fingerprints.

Skin has two layers. The thin, outer layer is the epidermis. It contains a tough, waterproof material called keratin. One page of this book is about the thickness of the epidermis over much of your body. The epidermis on the soles of feet is about twice as thick because it gets much more wear.

The dermis is the thicker, inner layer of the skin. The dermis contains blood vessels, nerve endings, sweat glands, and hair roots. Nerve endings allow you to feel texture, temperature, and pressure.

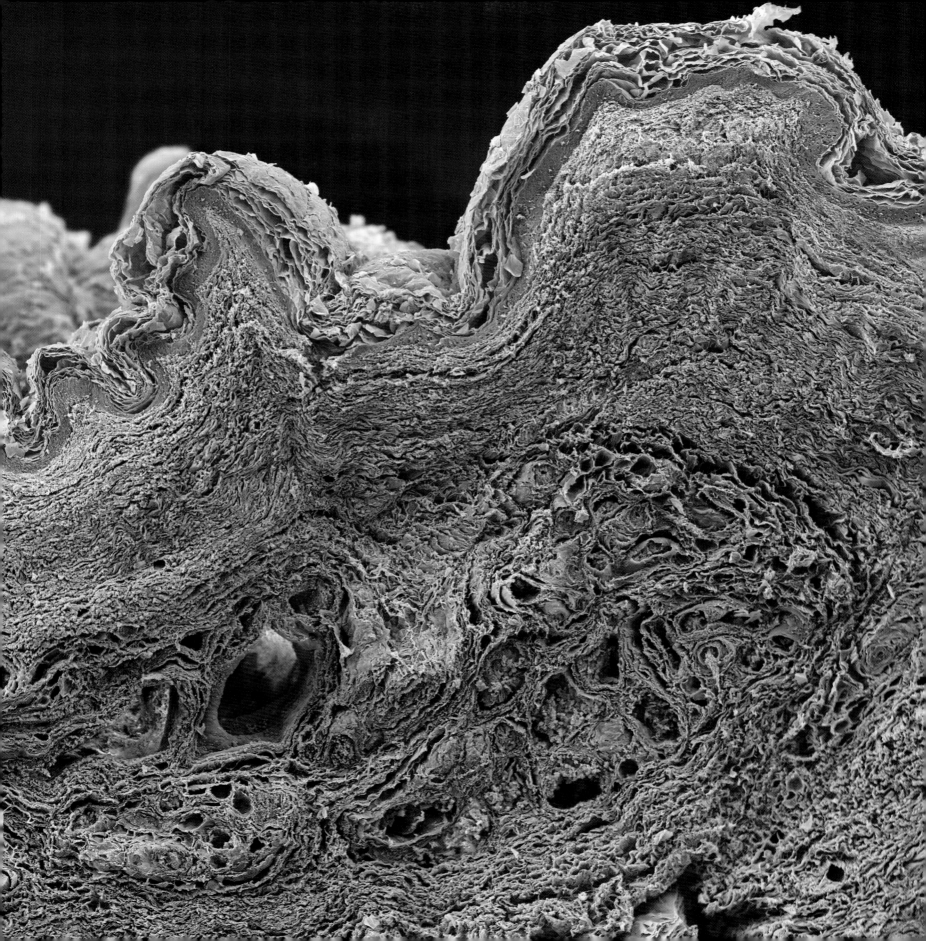

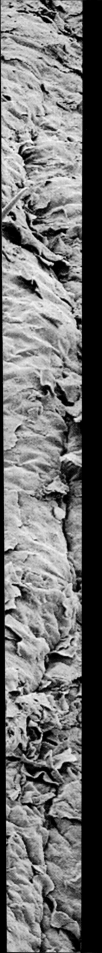

Hair and nails grow out of the skin. Nails are made of dead, flattened skin cells, toughened with keratin. They grow from living cells in the skin and protect the ends of fingers and toes. The body is covered with millions of hairs growing from roots in the dermis and pushing up through the epidermis. Thicker and longer hairs grow on the scalp protecting your head. Shorter, finer hairs cover the rest of the body. The hair on your head and body is not alive. That's why you can get a haircut and not feel pain.

Skin is the sense organ of touch. Nerve endings in the dermis send messages to the brain that signal pressure, pain, temperature changes, and the texture of things you touch. Fingertips have many more nerve endings than the skin over most of the rest of the body. That's why your fingertips can feel differences in pressure or heat so much more sensitively than your back can.

Melanin is the protective coloring matter in the skin. Dark skin has more melanin than light skin. Some people have freckles, little patches of skin with more melanin. Melanin increases with sunlight exposure and turns the skin darker.

The bones are like the framework of a building. Without the framework of beams and girders, a tall building would collapse. The bones in the body make up the skeleton. Without a skeleton, the body would collapse. If you didn't have a skeleton, you wouldn't be able to stand, walk, or run. Bones also protect important organs such as your brain, heart, and lungs.

There are about 206 bones in a human skeleton. When children are born, they have about 300 bones. As children grow into adults, some of the bones join, or fuse. Most bones have an outer layer that

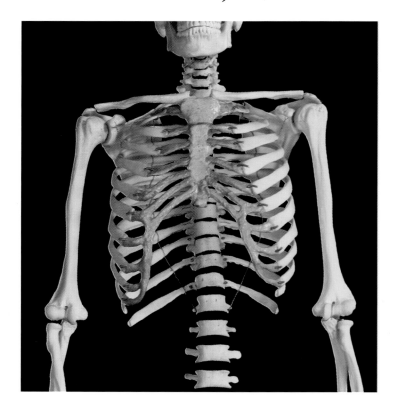

is dense and tough and is called hard bone. Inside the bone is a honeycomb of bone cells called spongy bone. The hollow centers of many bones are filled with marrow, a jellylike red and yellow substance. Each day, red **bone marrow** makes millions of red and white blood cells and a blood material called platelets.

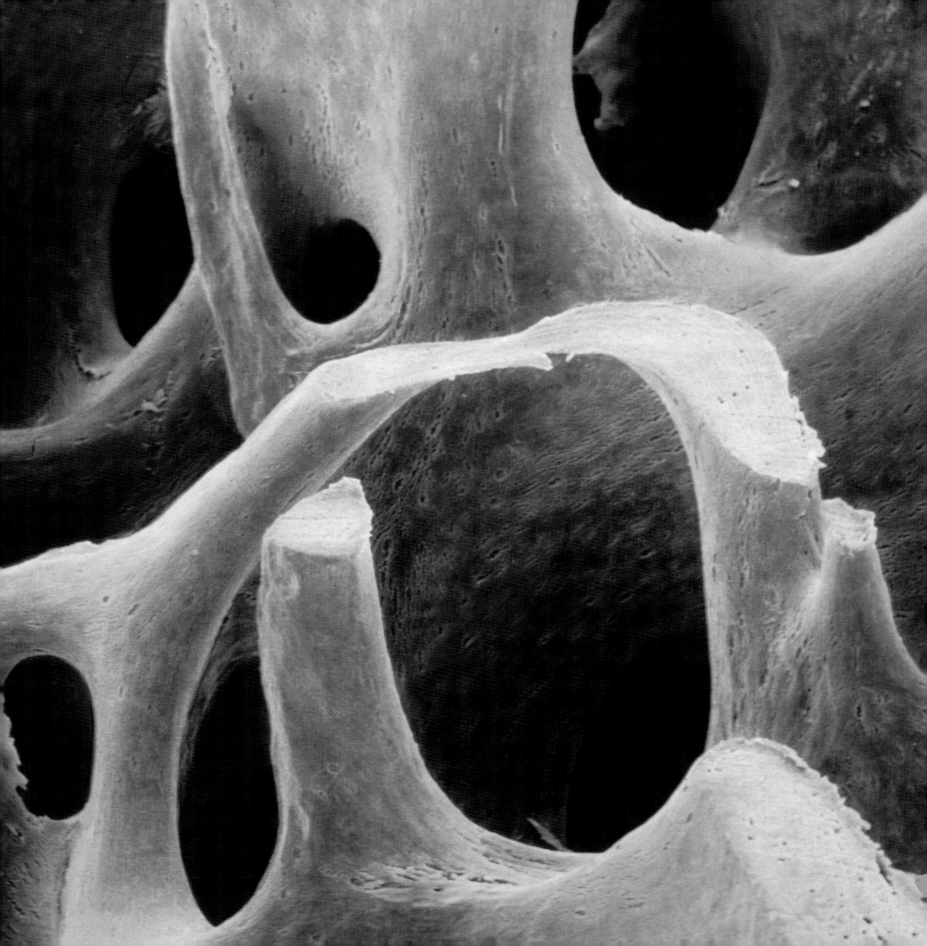

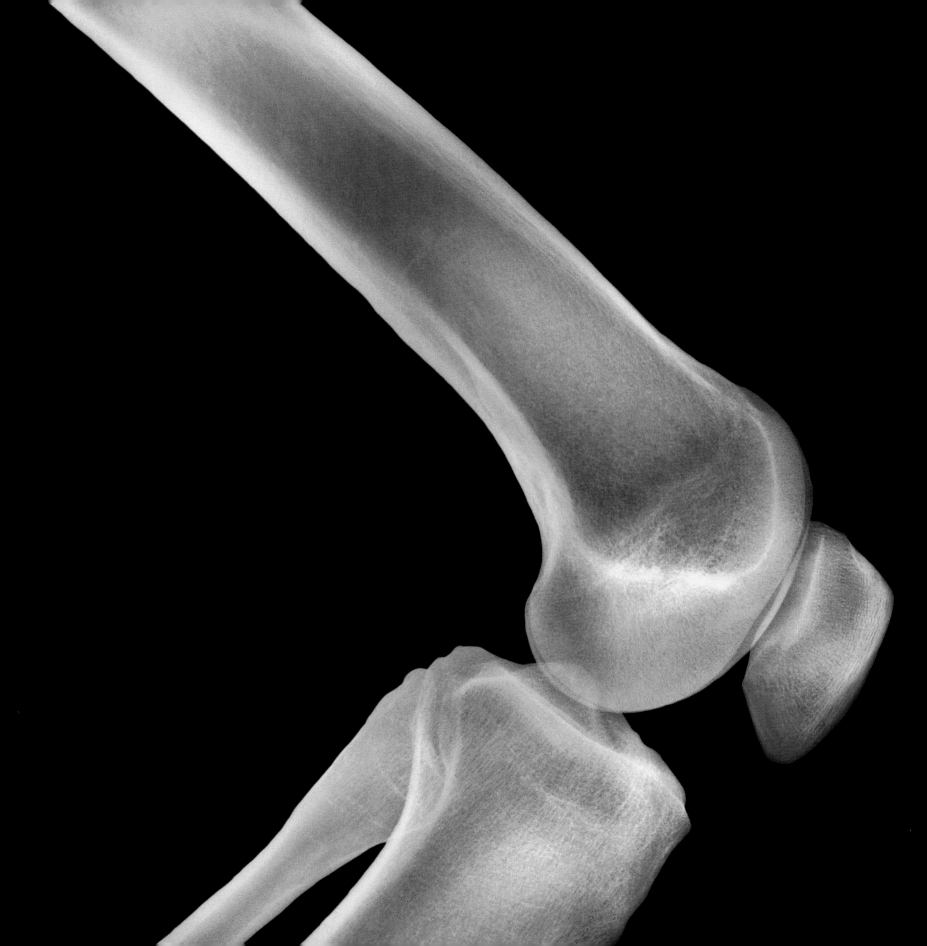

When bones come together, they form a joint. In some places, such as your skull, the bones are locked together. But most joints allow the bones to move easily against each other and are coated with a thick, slippery fluid like the oil on a door hinge. There are many kinds of moveable joints in the skeleton, such as ball-and-socket joints in the hip and shoulder and hinge joints in the elbows, knees, and fingers. If a joint is twisted too much, it is sprained or dislocated.

Bones are moved by muscles that are attached by tendons, which also link muscles to other muscles. Most tendons are shaped like narrow cables that stretch. Ligaments link bones together at joints. Ligaments are very strong and hold bones together so that they can barely move. Without ligaments, bones at joints would be easily dislocated.

Cartilage is another kind of connective tissue found in joints and at the ends of bones. Cartilage is smooth, tough, and flexible. Touch the tip of your nose or the top of your ear and you can feel one kind of cartilage.

Whenever a person walks, jumps, picks up a ball, or turns the pages of a book, muscles move the body. Even when a person is still, muscles are at work, moving the chest in and out during breathing and pushing digested food through the stomach and intestines. In addition to the 640 muscles that a person controls, there are many muscles that are not consciously controlled, such as the heart muscles that keep blood pumping through the body.

Muscles are made of bundles of long, thin cells called muscle fibers. A single muscle fiber is thinner than a human hair and can be up to a foot long. When a muscle relaxes, it lengthens or stretches. Each muscle fiber contains thinner threads called fibrils. A fibril is made up of strands of two kinds of proteins. Proteins are important chemicals that the body uses to make cells.

Muscles are controlled by electrical signals that come from nerves in the brain and spinal cord. When a muscle receives a nerve signal, it contracts and moves the part of the body to which it is attached. Muscles are often arranged in pairs, so that while one muscle pulls the bone one way, the other muscle relaxes.

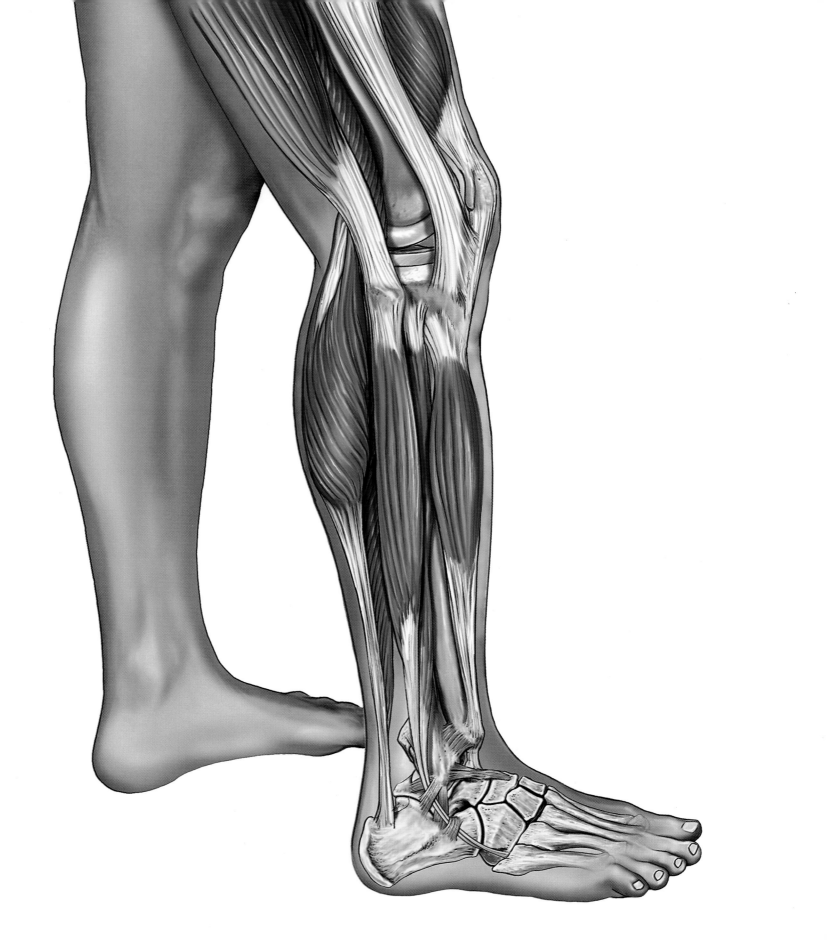

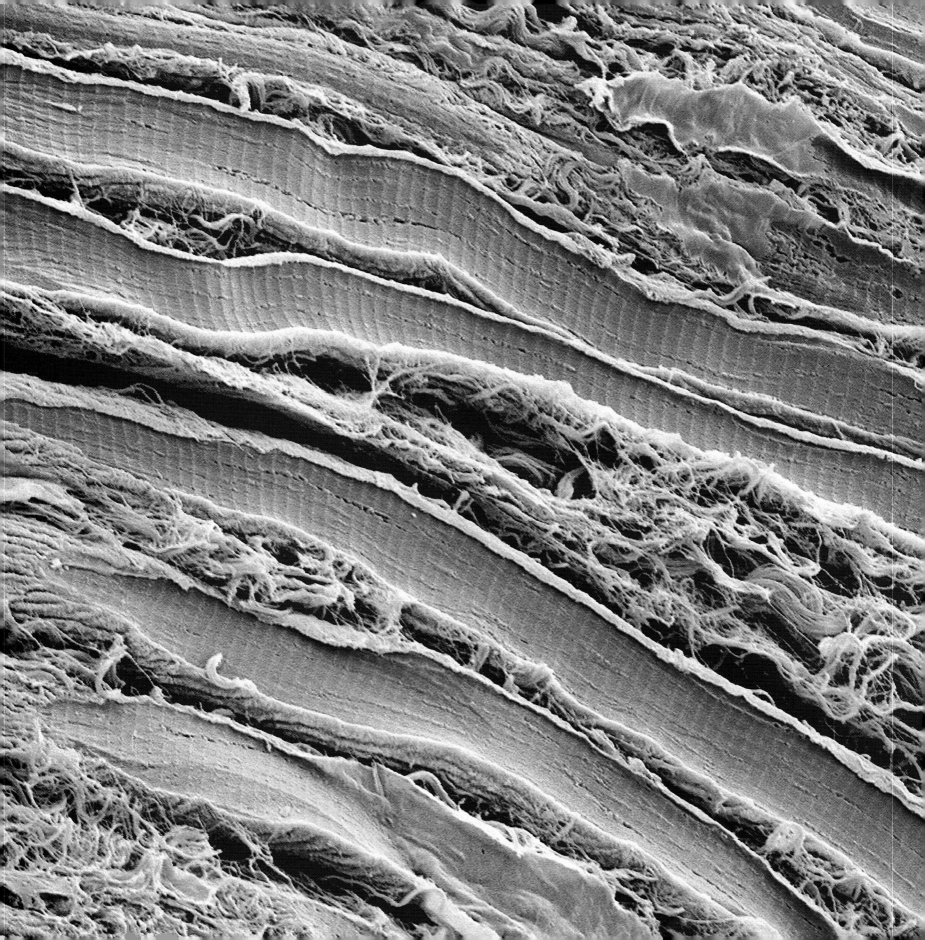

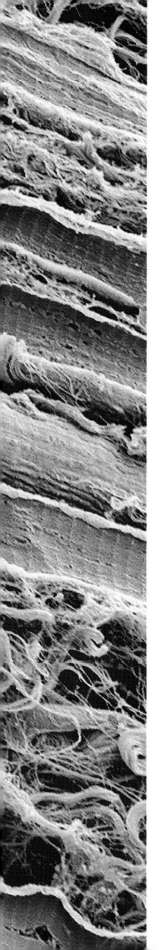

There are three kinds of muscles in the body. Muscles attached to bones are called skeletal muscles. Because they can be controlled, they are also called voluntary muscles. These muscles look striped, or striated, under a microscope.

Another kind of muscle is called smooth, or involuntary, muscle, because it cannot be consciously moved. Smooth muscles do not look striped under a microscope. Smooth muscles line the walls of the stomach, the intestines, and the blood vessels. These muscles contract the way skeletal muscles do but much more slowly and using less energy.

The heart is made up of cardiac muscle. Like smooth muscle, cardiac muscle is involuntary; you cannot consciously make your heart muscle contract. Cardiac muscle continually contracts and relaxes, pumping blood around the body sixty to seventy times a minute, one hundred thousand times a day. Cardiac muscle never tires the way skeletal muscle does.

Remember, the human body is made up of about a hundred trillion microscopic cells. The heart, blood vessels, and blood work together to supply the cells with all their needs. Twenty-four hours a day, the heart pushes a pulsing stream of blood through a network of blood vessels to the cells. The blood brings food and oxygen to each cell, carries away wastes, and helps protect the cells against disease. The heart, blood, and blood vessels compose the circulatory system.

Make a fist. That is about the size of your heart. The heart is in the middle of the chest, tilted slightly to the left. It is divided in half by a thick wall of muscles called the septum. Each half has two hollow chambers, one above the other.

Blood enters the heart in the upper chambers, the atria, which then pump the blood to the lower chambers, the ventricles. The ventricles are heavier and stronger than the atria. Each ventricle has a one-way valve to prevent blood from going backward.

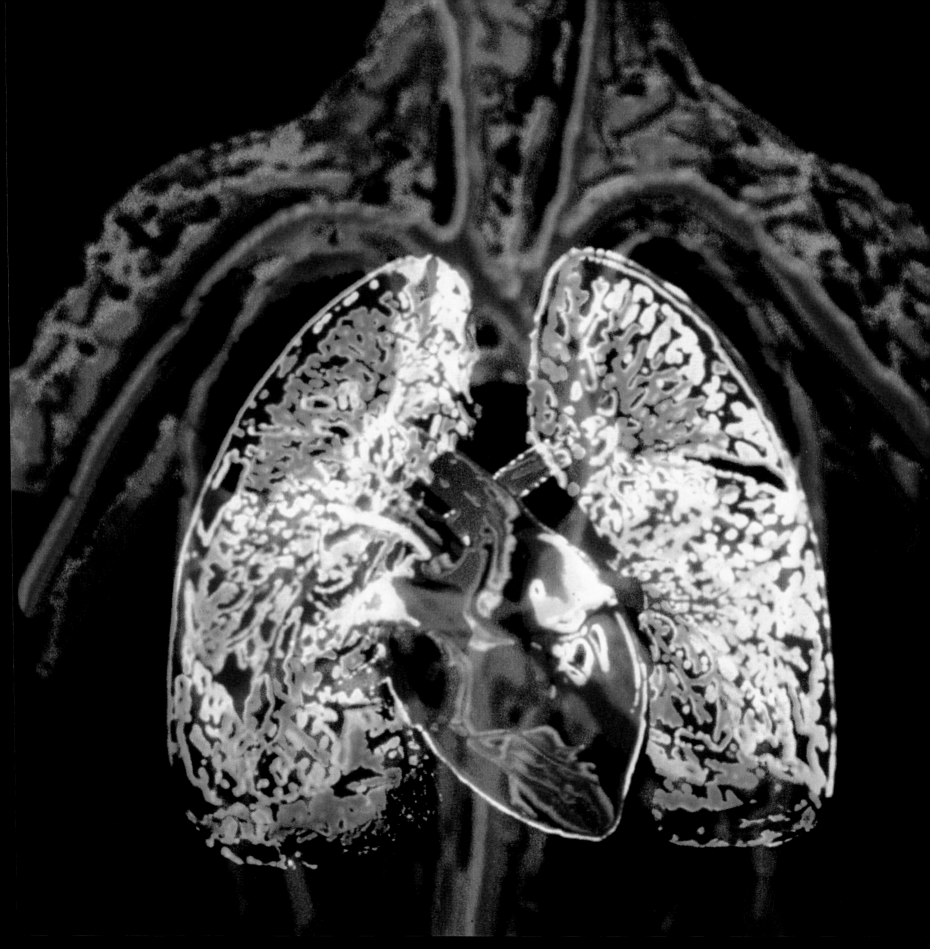

As blood pumps out of the left ventricle, it smashes with great force into the aorta, the largest blood vessel in the body. This begins a double journey that takes blood from the heart to every cell in the body, back to the heart, out to the lungs, and back again to the heart.

The aorta is an artery, a blood vessel that carries blood away from the heart. The walls of an artery are thick and strong. As they get farther away from the heart, arteries branch into arterioles, smaller and smaller vessels. Arterioles squeeze and relax regularly, forcing blood into billions of tiny capillaries that fan out all over the body.

The walls of capillaries are only one cell thick, thinner than a human hair. Oxygen and food nutrients pass from the blood through the thin capillary walls into the cells. At the same time, wastes move out of the cells and into the blood. Blood then passes from the capillaries into slightly larger blood vessels called venules, which join to form even larger blood vessels called veins. The largest veins are about as thick as a pencil. The bluish-looking blood vessels you see beneath your skin are veins. Veins have thinner walls than arteries do, and blood flows through them back to the heart in a steady current.

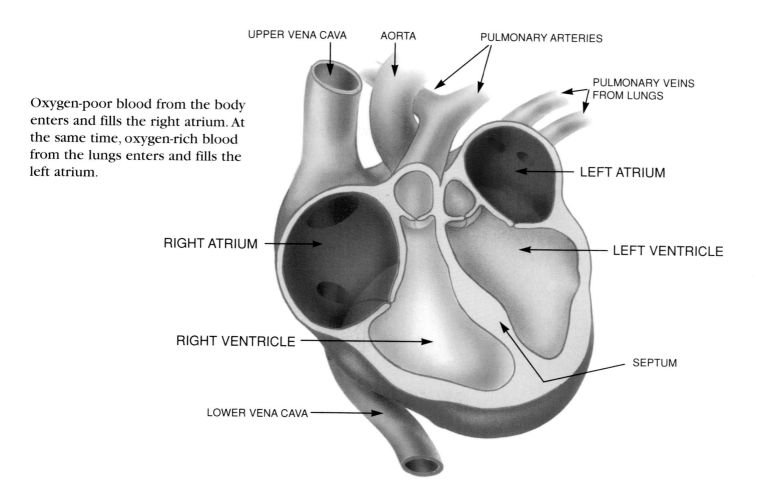

UPPER VENA CAVA

AORTA

PULMONARY ARTERIES

PULMONARY VEINS FROM LUNGS

LEFT ATRIUM

Oxygen-poor blood from the body enters and fills the right atrium. At the same time, oxygen-rich blood from the lungs enters and fills the left atrium.

RIGHT ATRIUM

LEFT VENTRICLE

RIGHT VENTRICLE

SEPTUM

LOWER VENA CAVA

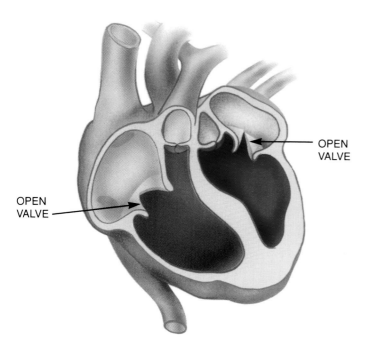

OPEN VALVE

OPEN VALVE

When the valves open, blood in the atria is pushed into the right and left ventricles.

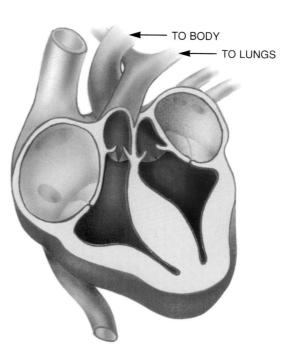

TO BODY

TO LUNGS

The right ventricle pushes blood to the lungs, and the left ventricle pumps blood out to the rest of the body.

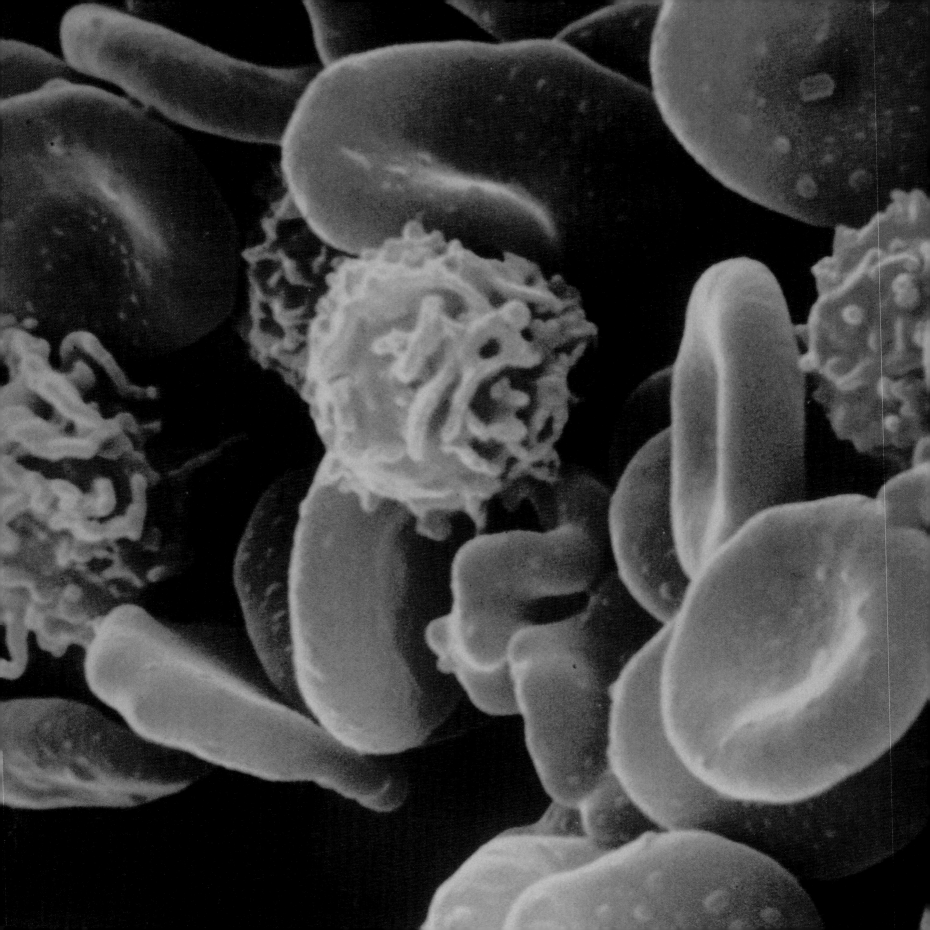

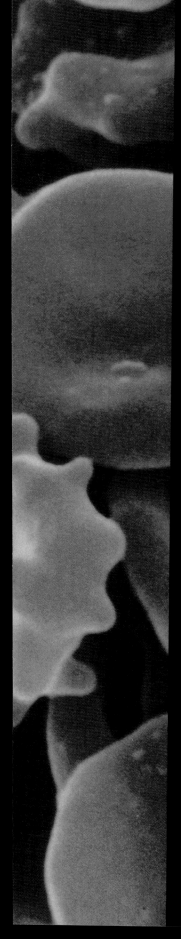

Blood is made up of red cells, white cells, and platelets, all floating in a clear, pale gold fluid called plasma. Plasma composes a little more than half of the blood.

Red blood cells are the most common cells in the human body. We each have about twenty-five trillion red blood cells, hundreds of times more red blood cells than there are stars in the Milky Way galaxy. Red blood cells contain the chemical **hemoglobin**, which carries oxygen from the lungs to the body's cells and then transports wastes such as **carbon dioxide** from the cells back to the lungs. Every second, special cells in the spongy tissue (marrow) of large bones make about three million blood cells, and in that same second an equal number die.

About one out of every seven hundred blood cells is a white blood cell. All the different kinds of white blood cells fight disease and infection.

Plasma also contains platelets, small disks that collect around a cut wherever bleeding occurs. The platelets help form clots that seal the cut and prevent further bleeding.

People may be able to go for days without food or water, but they can live for only a few minutes without air. The lungs and other parts of the respiratory system enable the body to inhale and exhale, to speak, to blow up a balloon, and to play a trumpet or a clarinet.

Inhalation is when air enters the nose or mouth and travels to the lungs. The nose is divided into two nostrils and opens into the nasal cavity. **Mucus**, a moist, sticky material, lines the nasal cavity and traps dust and germs. Air then travels into the throat, or pharynx. The voice box, or larynx, is at the bottom of the pharynx.

Below the voice box, air moves into the windpipe, or trachea.

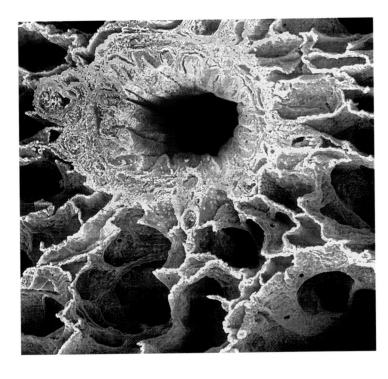 Toward the middle of the chest, the trachea splits into bronchi, two narrower tubes that go to each lung. Each bronchus splits into smaller bronchial tubes. Each air tube ends in a tiny bunch of air sacs called alveoli. The lungs contain more than six hundred million alveoli.

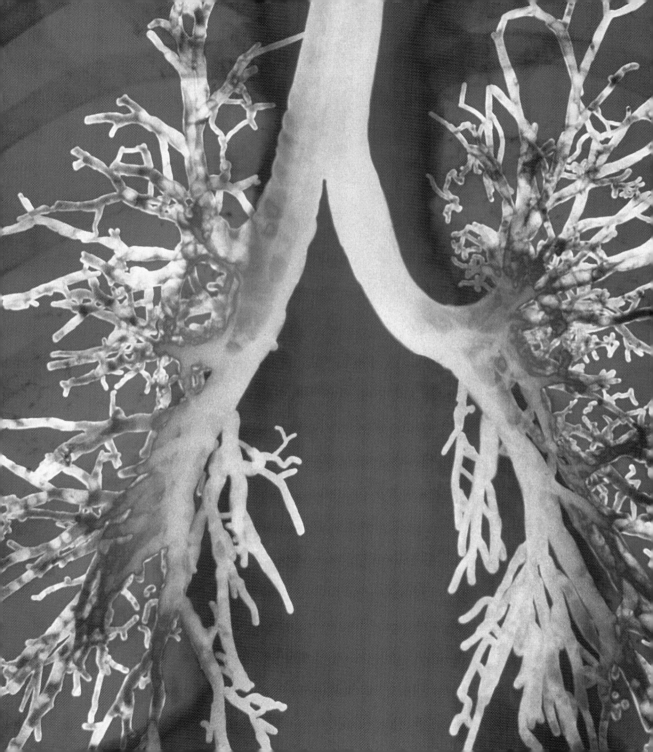

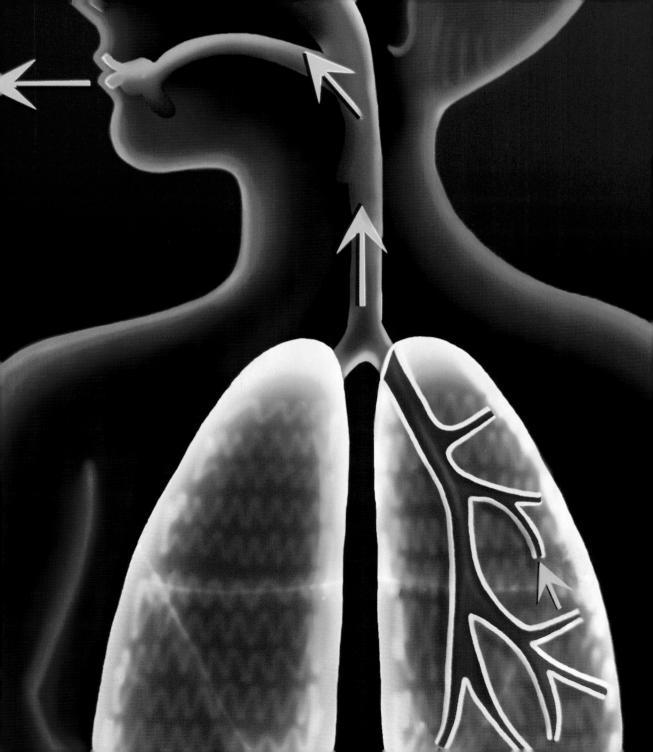

A network of small blood vessels surrounds each air sac. Oxygen and carbon dioxide pass through the walls of the air sac in either direction. A person inhales air with oxygen in it. When a person exhales, carbon dioxide exits the body and goes into the air.

The lungs take up most of the space inside the chest. Each lung is enclosed and protected in an airtight lining called a pleural sac. When resting, a person breathes in and out about ten to fifteen times a minute. During exercise, a person breathes more quickly and deeply.

The ribs, spinal column, breastbone, and all the muscles in between surround the chest and lungs. The diaphragm, a strong sheet of muscle, encloses the bottom of the chest. Every few seconds, the diaphragm moves downward, and the ribs and breastbone move forward and upward. That forces air inside the lungs and a person inhales. A few seconds later, the diaphragm relaxes and the ribs move downward. That forces air out of the lungs and a person exhales.

A person eats several hundred pounds of food in a year. The digestive system turns that truckload of bread, milk, fruits, vegetables, and pizza into the energy and nutrients a human body needs. Digestion takes place in a long tube called the gut, or digestive tract. The digestive tract begins in the mouth and runs through the **esophagus**, stomach, and small and large intestines. Finally, the body gets rid of undigested food through the anus. Food takes about forty hours to travel through the body.

People need to chew their food so that it can be swallowed and digested. Teeth are the hardest parts of the body. Chewing allows the hard teeth to crush and mash food and mix it with watery saliva, or spit. Saliva contains substances called **enzymes** that help break down food into nutrients the body can use.

The wet lump of chewed food in the mouth is called a bolus. The tongue pushes the bolus backward toward the throat. As soon as food is swallowed, everything else happens automatically.

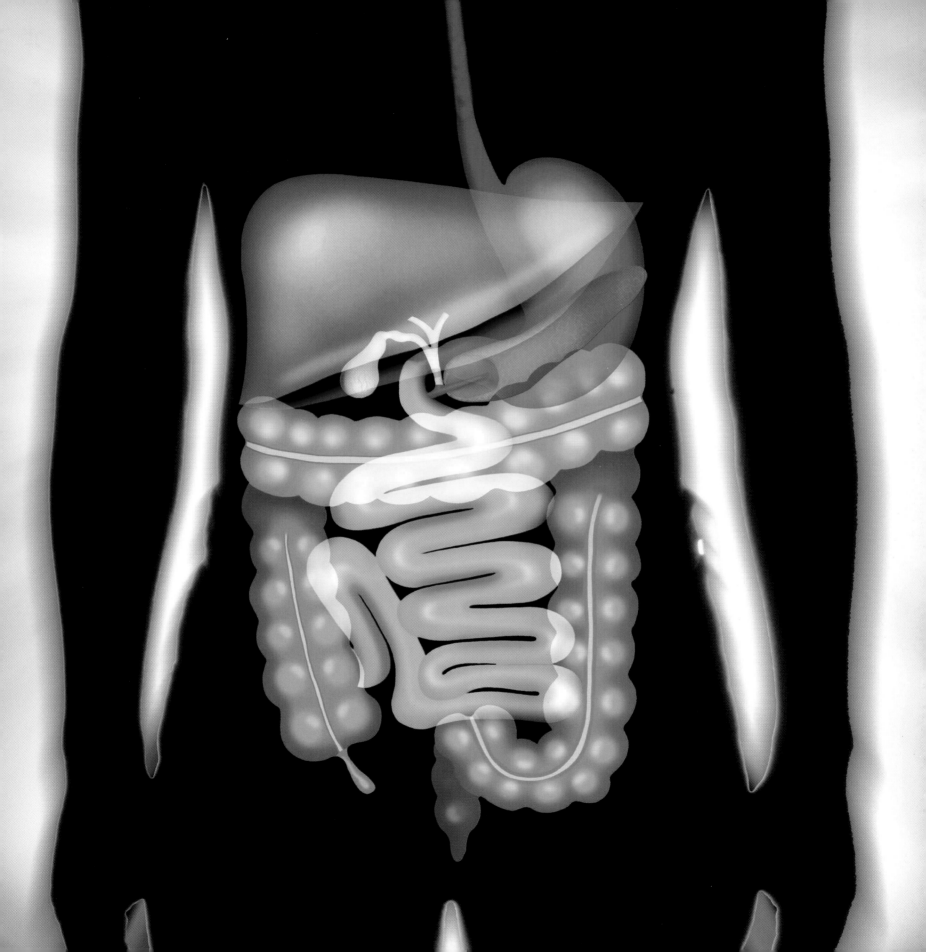

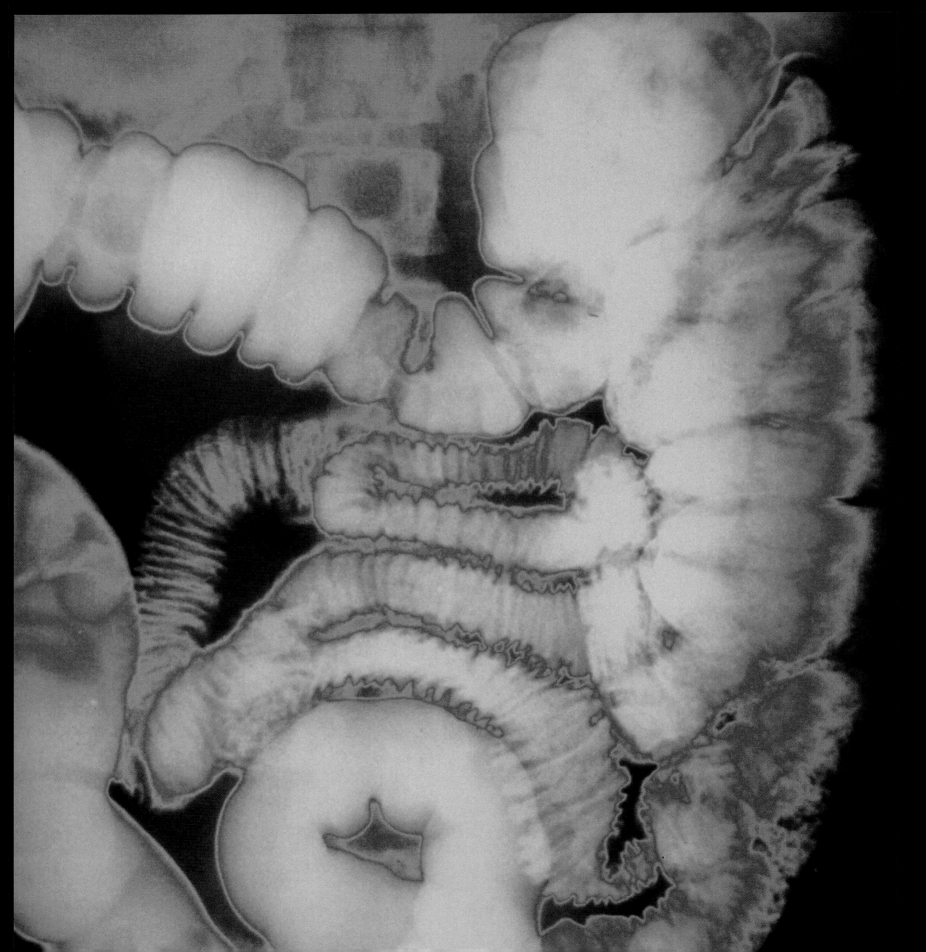

A tube called the esophagus leads down from the back of the throat to the stomach. Flaps, which open and close, prevent food from going up the nose or into the lungs. The muscles that line the esophagus contract and push the food along. This movement, called peristalsis, is similar to squeezing a tube of toothpaste. Slimy mucus coats the inside of the gut and makes it easier for the food to slip along the tube.

Chewed-up food leaves the esophagus and enters the stomach. The food is mixed with stomach, or gastric, juice. Three sets of muscles lining the stomach squeeze and tighten, mixing and churning the food inside. In about one to four hours, the food passes into the small intestine. The small intestine is about an inch and a half thick and twenty feet long. Most digestion happens as food travels through the twists and turns of the small intestine and the nutrients pass into the blood. Waste matter continues to travel into the large intestine and is excreted through the anus. Digestion is aided by juices produced by organs such as the liver and the pancreas, the body's chemical factories.

Special messenger cells called neurons carry signals back and forth from the brain to other parts of the body. Billions of neurons are linked in networks that make up the two main parts of the nervous system. The central nervous system, or CNS, consists of the brain and spinal cord. The network of neurons outside the brain is called the peripheral nervous system, or PNS.

A bundle of neurons is called a nerve. Nerves are the body's wiring. They carry tiny electrical-chemical signals called nerve impulses. Each second, millions of nerve signals travel from the brain to other parts of the body. This enables people to read, walk, laugh, breathe, say hello to a friend, or turn a page in a book.

The thinnest nerves are narrower than a hair. The thickest nerves look like pieces of white string. Messages leap from one nerve to the next across a tiny gap called a synapse. A synapse is about a millionth of an inch wide and is a kind of living switch. Nerve cells that respond to stimuli such as touch, sound, light, taste, temperature, and smell are called sensory neurons. Nerve cells that carry messages to muscle cells to make them move are called motor neurons.

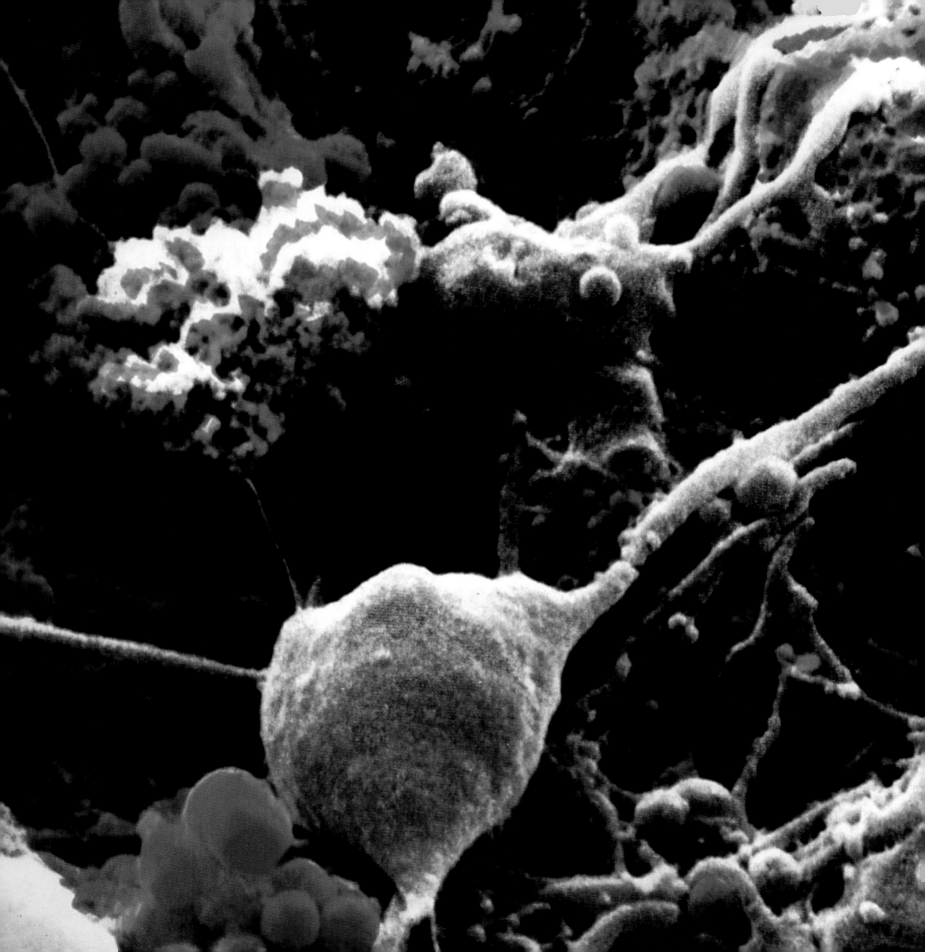

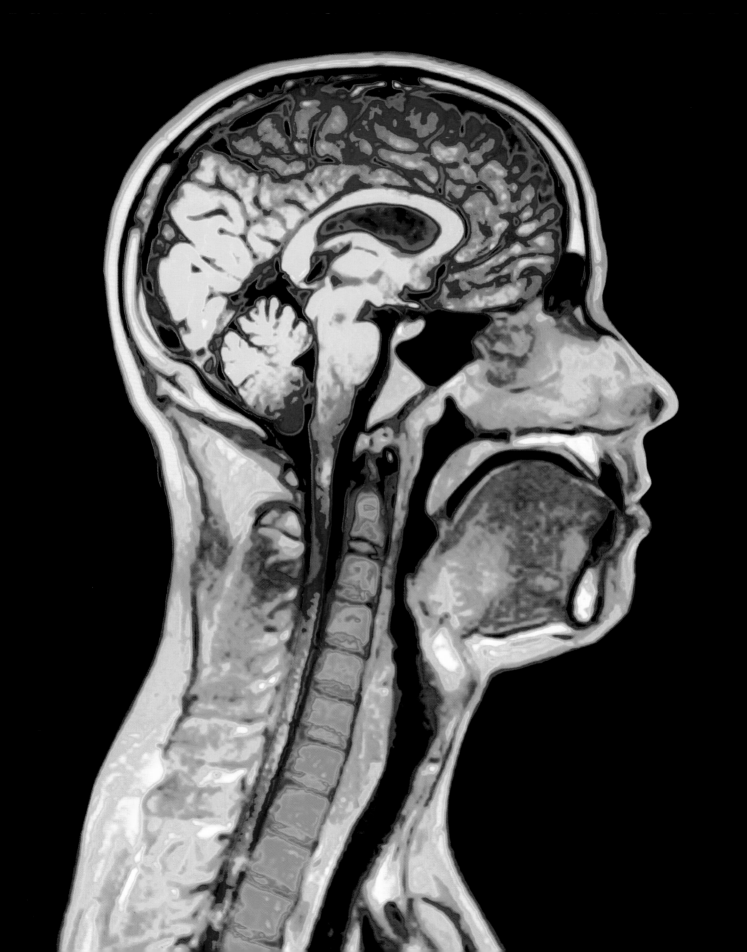

A human brain is about the size of a large grapefruit and weighs about three pounds when fully grown. It looks like a wrinkled blob of pinkish gray jelly. Eight bones fit together like the pieces of a jigsaw puzzle to form the skull that protects the brain. Inside the skull, the brain sits in a liquid bath that helps protect and cushion it against shocks.

The brain has three main sections: the cerebrum, the cerebellum, and the brain stem. The cerebrum is the "thinking brain," in which language, memory, and decision making are located. The deeply wrinkled surface of the cerebrum is called the cerebral cortex. The cortex is made up of ten billion to fourteen billion neurons. The cerebellum is the brain center for muscle movement, posture, and coordination. The brain stem regulates automatic functions, such as heartbeat, blood pressure, breathing, and digestion.

The spinal cord lies below the brain stem. It is the main nerve pathway between the brain and the rest of the body. The spine, composed of thirty-three separate bones called vertebrae, helps protect the spinal cord from injury.

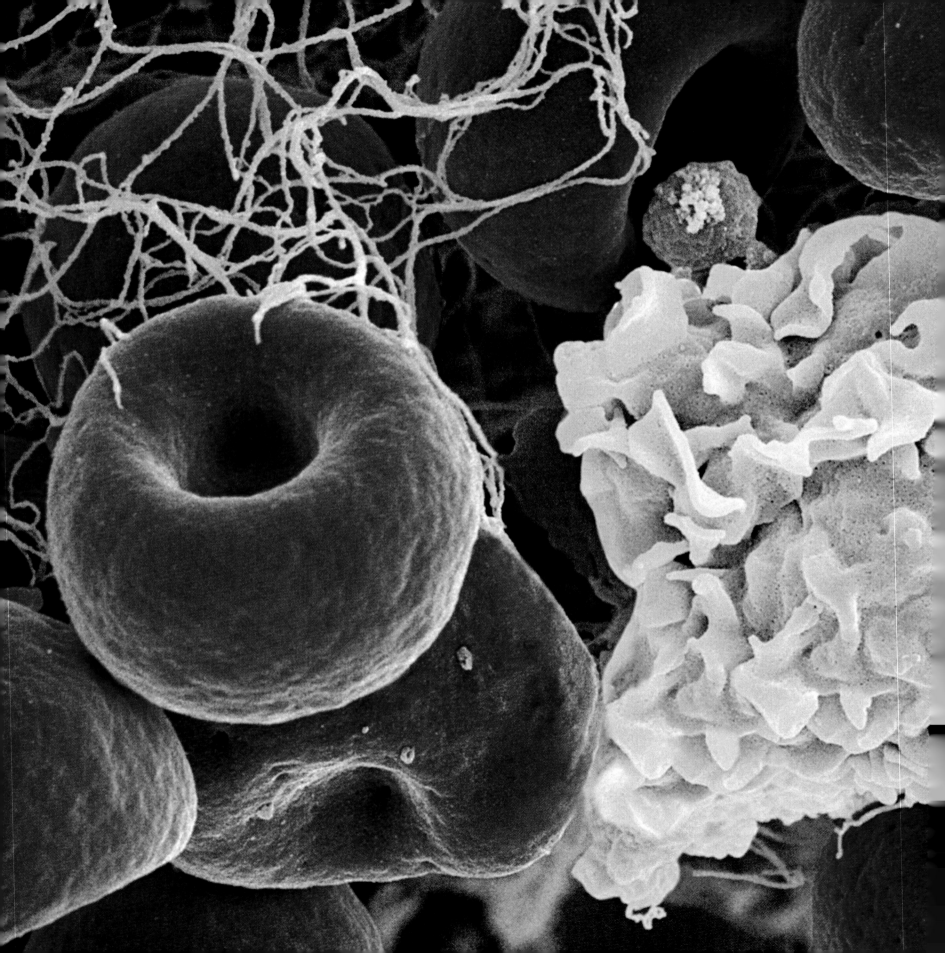

The body's first line of defense against infection and harmful germs and viruses is called the immune, or lymphatic, system. Lymph, a clear fluid containing mostly white blood cells, bathes the cells and tissues of the body.

Lymph nodes, small groups of lymph tissue, dot the network of lymph vessels. The nodes contain white blood cells that attack germs and act as a filter for the lymph passing through. When the nodes are fighting infection, they sometimes swell up and are called "swollen glands."

The **spleen**, **thymus**, and bone marrow help fight disease. They produce antibodies that are able to recognize and attack different kinds of disease germs. The immune system destroys most infections. Immunization, provided by a vaccine, boosts the immune system against a particular type of infection, including measles and chicken pox.

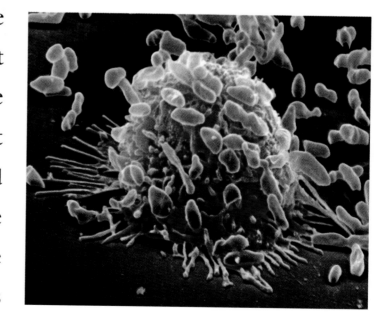

The excretory system is the system that rids the body of waste. This includes solid wastes that pass through the large intestine and liquid wastes that are produced in the kidneys. Some liquid wastes also evaporate from the skin as sweat (which helps cool the body), and some leave through the lungs, which you can see as breath that condenses on a cold day.

The kidneys, the bladder, and its connecting tubes make up the urinary system. The kidneys are bean-shaped organs that filter the blood and remove waste products such as urea as well as excess water. Urea and excess water form about two to three pints of urine that is squeezed down tubes and stored in the muscular bladder.

The body is made up of about 60 percent water. If the body has too much water, it would be bloated. If it has too little water, the body would become dehydrated. The excretory system balances the amount of water excreted with the amount of water kept in the body.

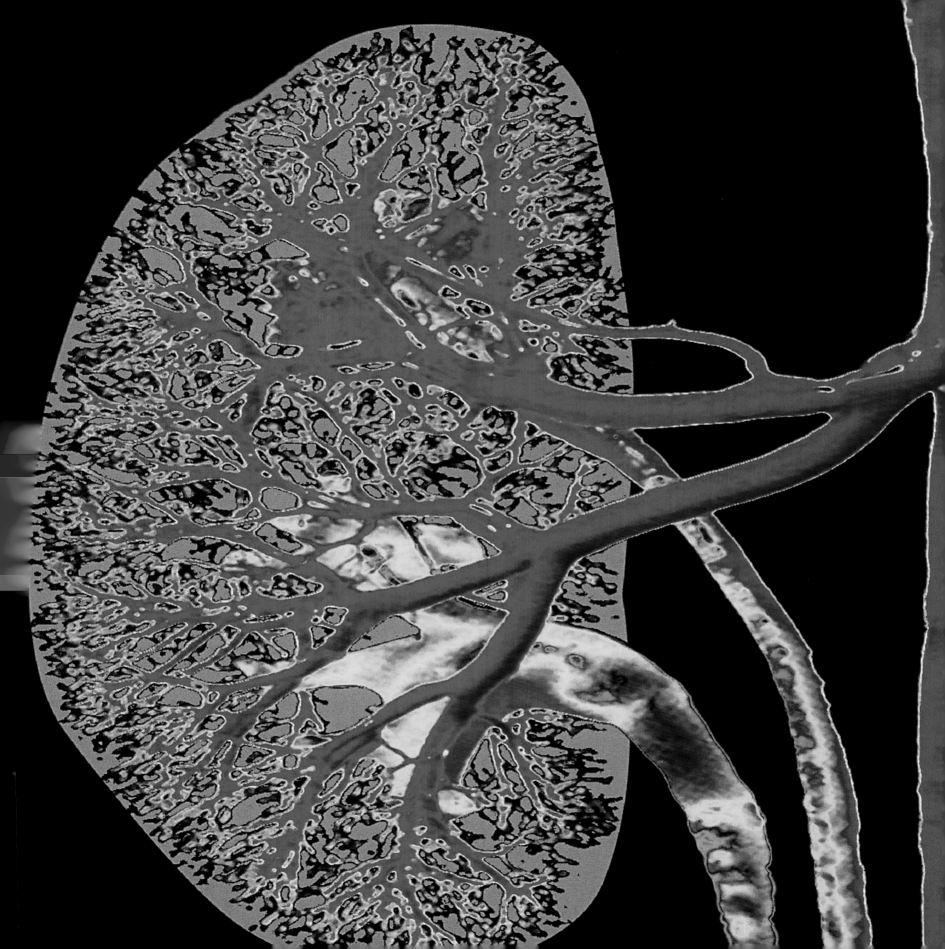

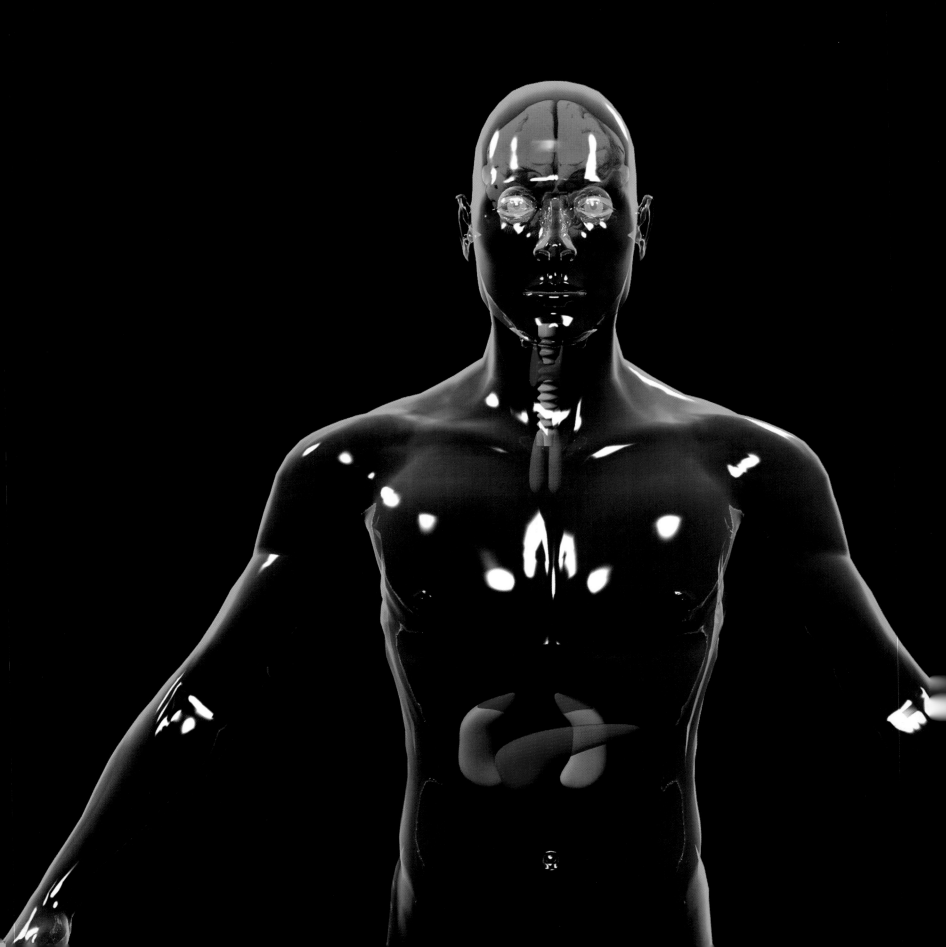

The endocrine system controls many of the body's slower activities, such as growth. Faster activities, such as breathing and movement, are controlled by the nervous system. Both systems work together to keep the body functioning properly.

The endocrine system is made up of special cells and tissues, called glands, and **hormones**, the chemical messengers glands produce. The pituitary, a pea-sized gland located in the head, is the master gland. It produces hormones that directly regulate body activities and hormones that control other glands. Other glands in the body are the thyroid, the parathyroids, the adrenals, the pancreas, the pineals, and the reproductive glands.

Endocrine glands produce more than twenty important hormones that are carried to cells all over the body via the bloodstream. Each hormone affects only particular kinds of cells. Some of the hormones in the body include growth hormones, endorphins that act on the nervous system, and hormones that control your metabolism. Hormones also help control blood pressure, heart rate, and the body's response to stress.

The cells and organs of the body that make new individuals are called the reproductive system. With people and most other mammals, the baby develops inside the female's uterus. After the baby is born, it feeds on milk produced in the mother's mammary glands.

Each of the two sexes, female and male, has a different role in reproduction. The reproductive system in each is present during childhood but is not developed and not functional until adulthood. The change from a child into an adult, usually in the teenage years,

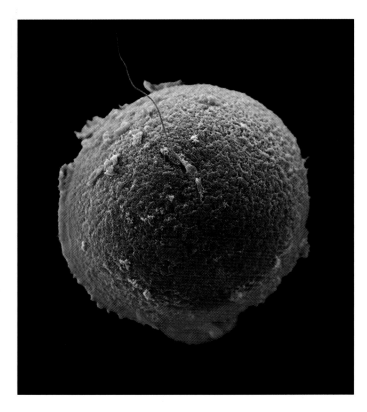

is called puberty.

After puberty, female reproductive organs, the ovaries, produce egg cells. Male reproductive parts, or testes, create sperm cells. During fertilization, a sperm cell is transferred to the female's body and unites with an egg cell. Pregnancy is when the fertilized egg develops within the mother.

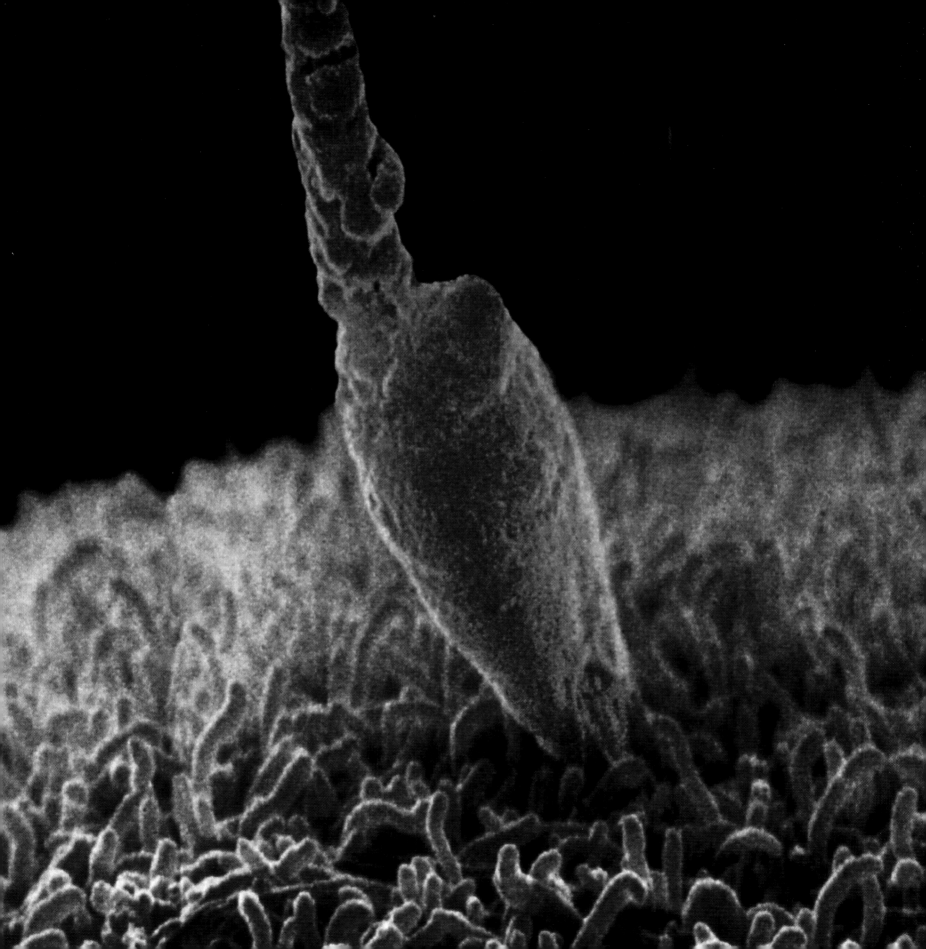

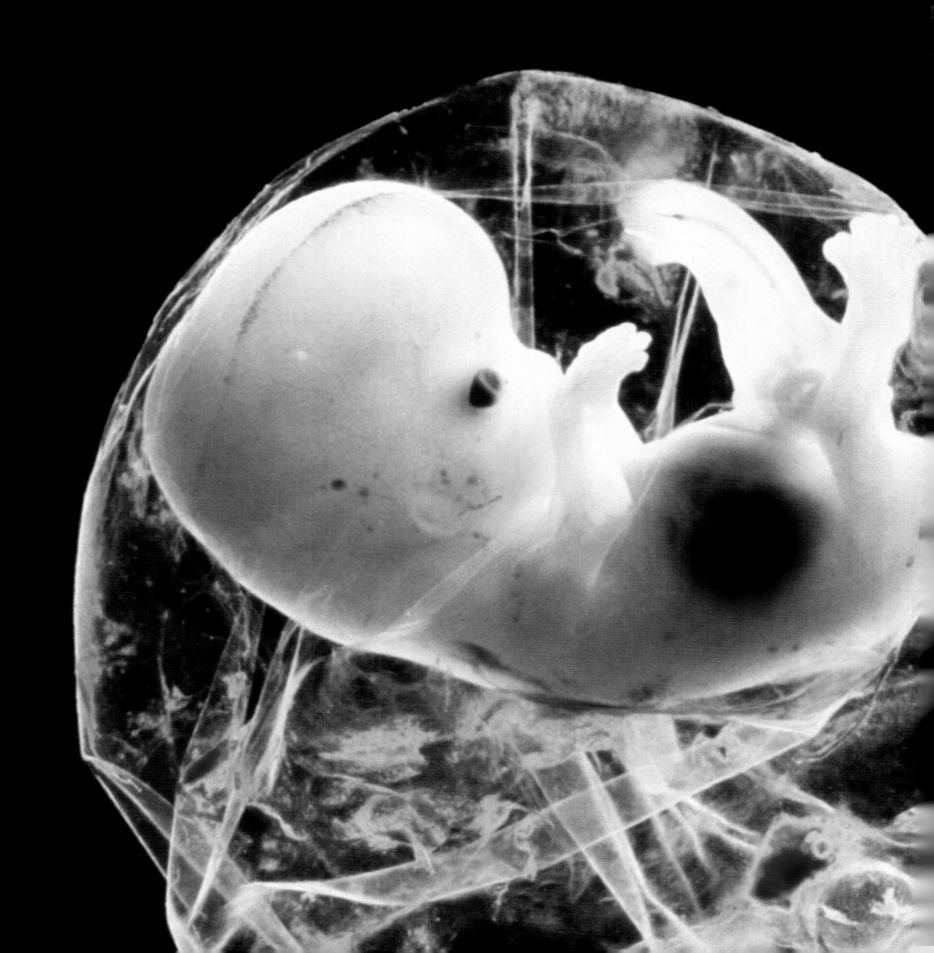

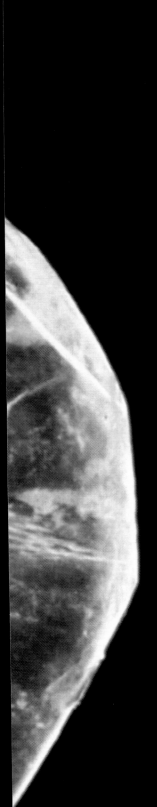

During the beginning weeks of development, the new individual is called an embryo. After about two months, the embryo develops into a fetus. The fetus receives oxygen and food from the mother through the placenta and the umbilical cord. The placenta is a tissue that lines the inner surface of the uterus. The umbilical cord carries blood between the fetus and the placenta.

After about nine months, a baby is fully developed inside the placenta. The baby is born when it is pushed out from the uterus through the birth canal. Once the baby is born, it begins to cry and it starts breathing. The umbilical cord is clamped shut and cut. The baby is a separate individual.

At first, a newborn sleeps most of the time except to nurse. After a few weeks, the baby begins to smile and reacts to its parent and surroundings. At about eight or nine months, the growing child begins to crawl and tries to stand. After about a year, a child begins to talk and communicate using language.

Why do new babies look like their mother and their father? The reason lies inside the DNA in every one of the body's trillions of cells.

DNA (deoxyribonucleic acid) is a long, double-spiral chemical that is different for every person who ever existed.

Small sections of DNA called genes contain body-building instructions that make each baby unique. Every baby gets two sets of genes, one from its mother and one from its father. The information in the

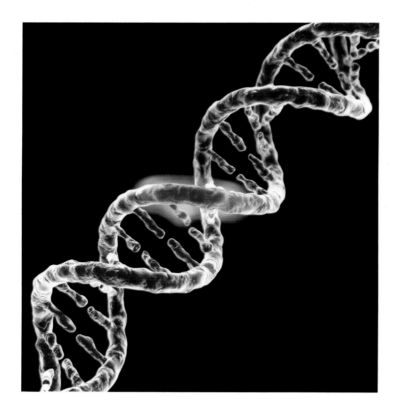

genes determines the physical characteristics of each baby—from eye and skin color to height and hand size to whether the baby is a girl or a boy. Identical human twins and triplets share the same genes. That's why they look so much alike. Everyone else in the world has a unique set of genes.

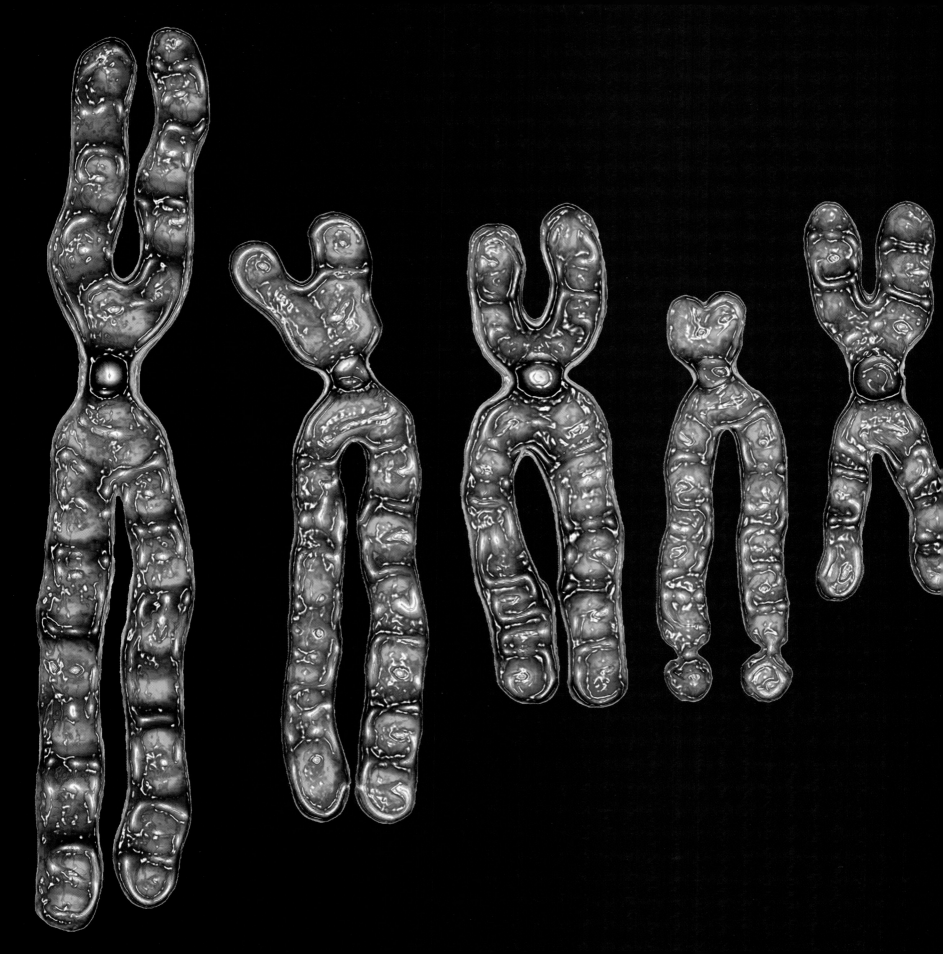

Light comes from many different sources, including the sun and electric bulbs. How do we see things with our eyes?

Our two eyeballs sit in cuplike sockets in the front of the head. Rays of light enter the eyeball through the cornea. The cornea acts like a camera lens and bends light into the eye. The iris is the colored part of the eye behind the cornea. The pupil is the opening in the iris. The cornea focuses light through the pupil onto the back of the eye, the retina.

Light-sensitive cells in the retina are connected to the brain by a large optic nerve. It carries information to a relay system of nerve fibers in the brain. The information compiled from each eye travels to the opposite side of the brain. The brain puts together nerve impulses from the eyes, and the person sees what's out there.

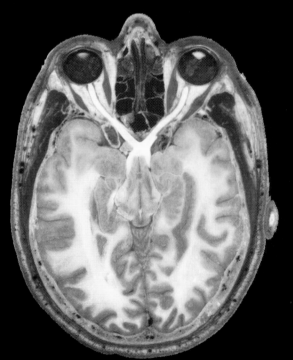

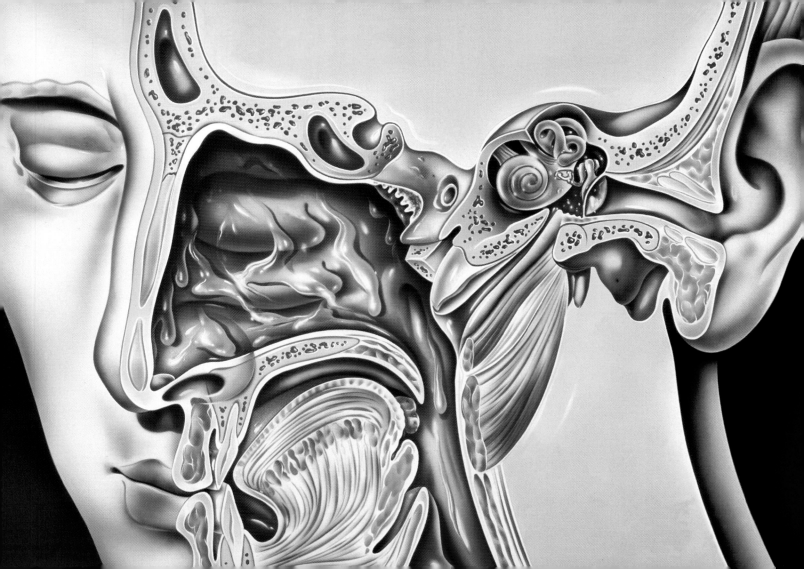

A human ear has three parts: the outer ear, the middle ear, and the inner ear. The outer ear is a sound catcher. It funnels sound waves down a short tube to the **eardrum**. The eardrum separates the outer ear from the middle ear.

Sound waves cause the eardrum to vibrate just like the top of a drum when it is hit by a drumstick. Inside the middle ear are the three smallest bones of the body, called the hammer, the anvil, and the stirrup. Vibrations of the eardrum cause the bones to move, and the motion is transmitted to another tight flap of skin, called the oval window.

The inner ear lies in a bony hollow in the skull and is a maze of spaces ending in a coiled spiral tube, called the cochlea. Nerve cells in the cochlea send a message through the auditory nerve to the hearing centers in the brain.

Next to the cochlea are three semicircular canals. These help keep a person balanced when sitting, walking, jumping, and bending.

Taste and smell are linked together because both depend upon similar kinds of nerve endings that can detect chemicals. Taste buds are the nerve receptors for taste in the mouth. Olfactory nerves, in the back of the nose, are the receptors for smell. Taste and smell allow people to tell one kind of food from another, identify different odors, and avoid bitter or sour smells or tastes that might be dangerous.

People recognize odors because each different odor molecule fits into an olfactory nerve cell the way a key fits into a lock. The cells send signals along the olfactory nerve to the brain, where each smell is identified. Humans can distinguish between 4,000 and 10,000 odors, including such diverse aromas as perfume, mint gum, vinegar, and mothballs.

Taste is the weakest of the five senses and ten thousand times less sensitive than smell. The tongue and the roof of the mouth are covered with thousands of tiny taste buds that recognize sweet, salty, sour, and bitter tastes.

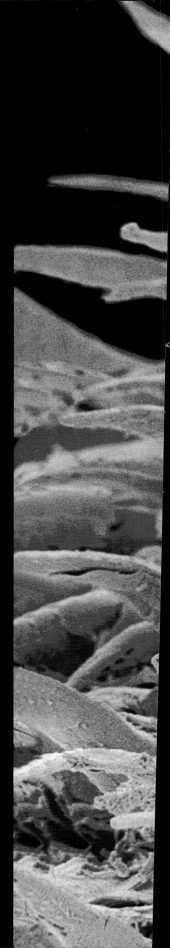

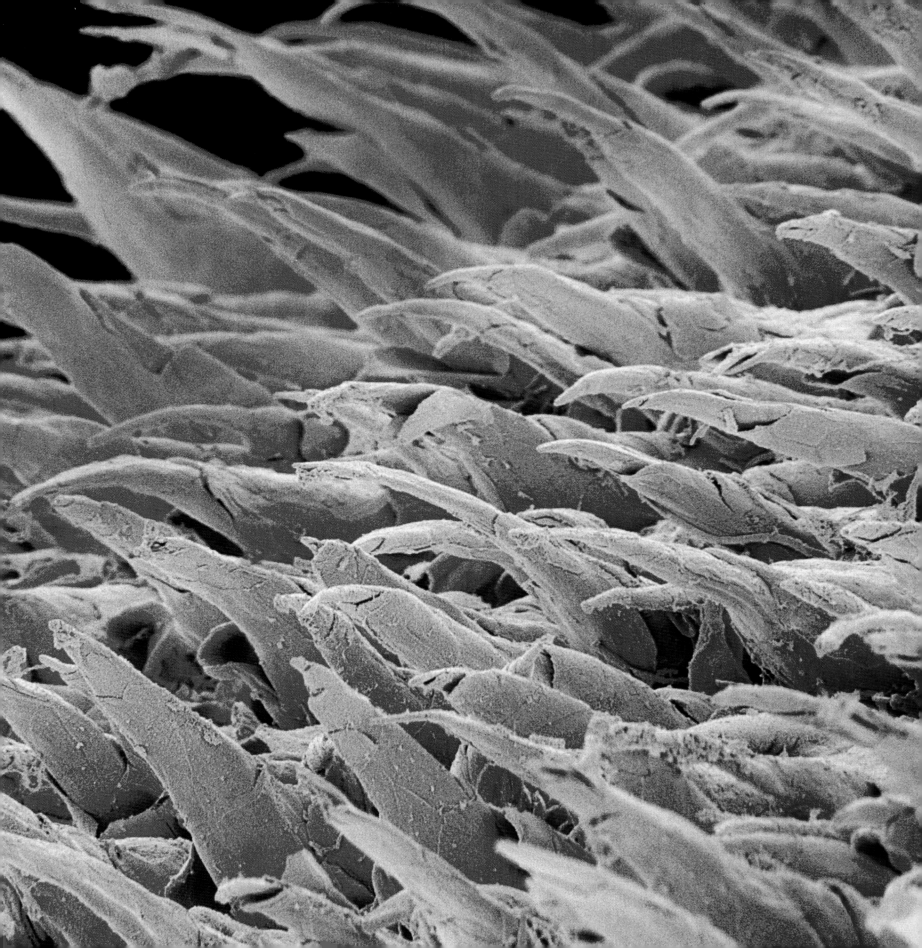

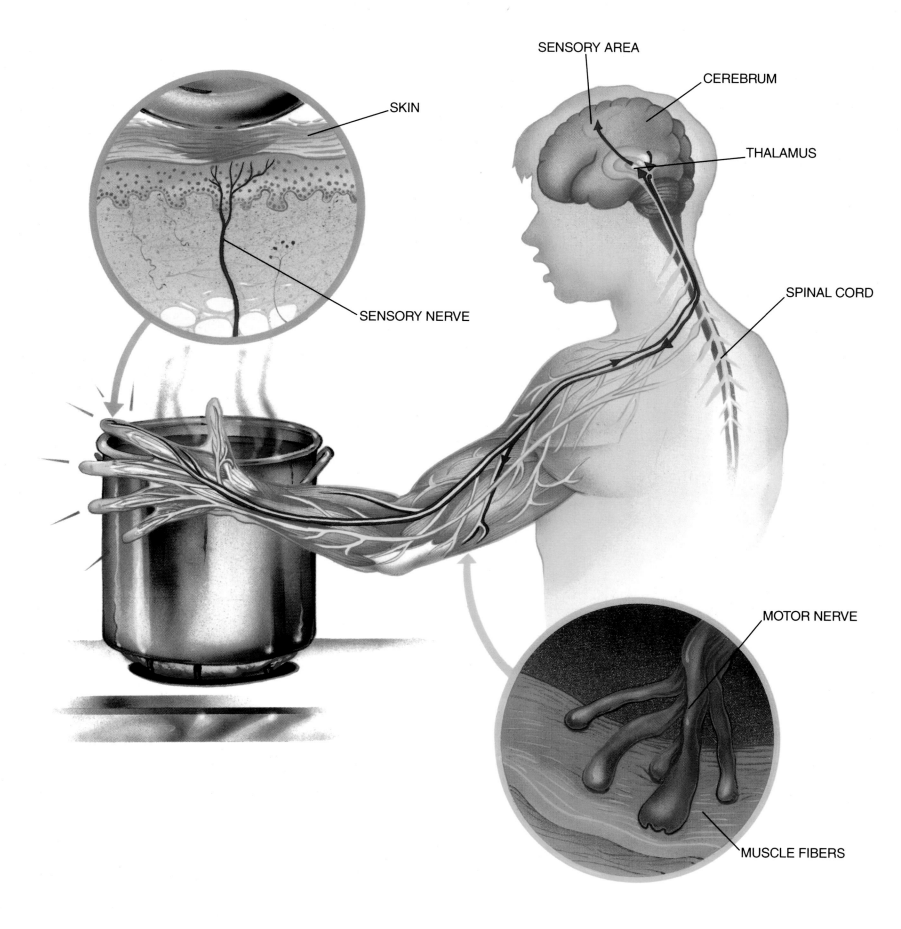

SKIN

SENSORY NERVE

SENSORY AREA

CEREBRUM

THALAMUS

SPINAL CORD

MOTOR NERVE

MUSCLE FIBERS

The senses of sight, hearing, taste, and smell are located in particular parts of the body, but the sense of touch is in the skin all over the body. The feelings of touch begin in the dermis, the bottom layer of skin. The dermis is filled by many tiny nerve endings that give information about the things the body touches. The nerves carry the messages to the spinal cord, which then sends messages to the brain, and a person feels the appropriate sensation.

About twenty different kinds of nerve endings in the skin are sensitive to many different sensations. The most common nerve receptors are those for pain, heat, cold, and pressure or touch.

Some parts of the body are more sensitive than others because they have more nerve endings. The fingers are far more sensitive to touch than the back. People who are blind or visually impaired use their sensitive fingertips when they read Braille, a reading system that uses patterns of raised dots on a page. The feet, face, neck, and tongue are also very sensitive to touch. That's why it hurts so much when you accidentally bite your tongue.

Every human being goes through the same stages of life:

• Infancy is marked by rapid growth and skill learning, such as crawling and making sounds.

• Childhood begins with the ability to talk and walk, and then learning to read, write, and interact with other people.

• Adolescence begins between ages ten and twelve for girls and between twelve and fourteen for boys. Bodies grow rapidly into adult shapes for women and men.

• Adulthood: Humans in their twenties and thirties are at their physical peak. Most athletes excel in sports during those years.

• Middle age occurs in the forties and fifties and old age begins in the late fifties and early sixties. Wrinkles appear, hair thins and grays, and the senses dull.

With the help of sophisticated medicine, exercise, and proper **nutrition**, the amazing human body has become even more durable. Although old age begins in the early sixties, people are living longer than ever before.

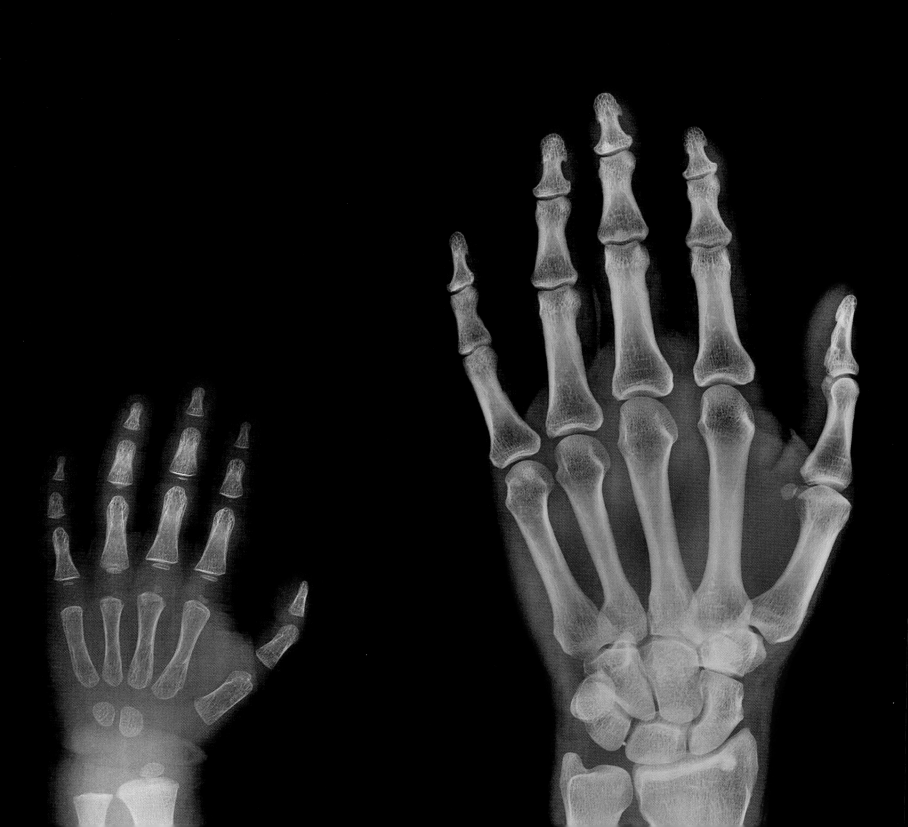

GLOSSARY

Bone marrow—Soft tissue found in the cavities of most bones; essential to the immune system.

Carbon dioxide—A colorless, odorless gas the body gets rid of during exhalation.

Cartilage—Flexible connective tissue that covers the ends of bones in a joint.

Cell—The smallest unit of life.

Eardrum—A thin membrane that covers the ear cavity and receives sound waves.

Enzyme—A chemical that assists reactions in the body; essential to the digestive system.

Esophagus—A muscular tube in the throat that forces food down to the rest of the digestive system.

Hemoglobin—A chemical in the blood that transports oxygen and iron around the body.

Hormone—A chemical made by the body to stimulate certain changes and activities.

Mucus—A slippery substance that protects and moistens various parts inside the body.

Nutrition—The use of food to fuel and maintain the body.

Organ—A structure made of tissue that has a specific function in the body.

Spleen—An organ near the stomach that destroys unneeded red blood cells; essential to the immune system.

Thymus—Tissue structure that functions in the development of the body's immune system.

Tissue—A group of cells of a particular kind that forms many of the body's structures.

X-ray—The process of using electromagnetic waves to look inside the body without having to cut it open.

INDEX

IMAGES

page 3: A medical illustration that shows the muscles of the body and their placement over bone.

page 4: A colored X-ray of a human skull. The fused bones of the cranium (center) encase and protect the brain.

page 5: A colored magnetic resonance imaging (MRI) scan of the entire body of a man in coronal (frontal) section.

page 7: A false-color scan of a fat-storing cell.

pages 8–9: A digital composite showing a man's organs and vascular system.

page 10: A colored scanning electron microscope (SEM) image of the epidermis, the outermost layer of human skin.

page 11: A microscopic image of a cross section of human skin.

page 12: A colored SEM image shows hairs on a person's upper lip.

page 14: Frontal view of the human skeleton, showing the base of the skull, sternum, ribs, collar bone, and upper limbs.

page 15: A false-color SEM micrograph of spongy bone tissue.

page 16: A colored X-ray of the healthy knee joint of an adult woman, seen from the side.

page 19: A medical illustration of the muscles of the right leg and some bones of the right foot.

page 20: A colored SEM micrograph of skeletal muscle fibers.

page 23: A computer-colored scan of the chest shows the lungs, heart, and pulmonary circulation.

page 26: A computer-colored SEM micrograph that shows blood cells magnified thousands of times.

page 28: Bronchial tubes and alveoli in a human lung.

page 29: A colored chest X-ray showing the healthy airways (red) of the lungs, including the trachea (windpipe, upper center) that divides into two main bronchi, which enter each lung. The bronchi then split further into smaller bronchi.

page 30: The path air takes through the lungs and out the mouth during exhalation, which rids the body of carbon dioxide.

page 33: An illustration of the digestive system's major organs: stomach, liver, pancreas, gall bladder, small intestine, and large intestine.

page 34: A colored X-ray image of the human abdomen, showing the large intestine. At center are loops of the small intestine.

page 37: A computer-colored SEM micrograph shows neurons (grayish white) and glial cells (red-orange) that provide support and nutrition to the nervous system, magnified over 20,000 times.

page 38: A colored scan of the brain and nervous system that clearly shows the spinal cord.

page 40: A colored SEM micrograph of red blood cells and a white blood cell; some fibrin, a protein that functions in blood clotting, is also shown.

page 41: White blood cells attack a bacterial infection.

page 43: A colored X-ray of a healthy kidney.

page 44: Computer artwork showing the male body's endocrine system.

The glands are colored red.

page 46: A color-enhanced SEM micrograph of a human ovum being fertilized by a sperm.

page 47: A colored SEM micrograph of a single sperm fertilizing a human egg.

page 48: A human fetus at 6 weeks of development. Eyes and limbs are visible.

page 50: A computer-generated model of human DNA.

page 51: Five human chromosomes. A human chromosome contains the genes that determine a person's physical characteristics, including gender.

page 52: A false-color SEM micrograph of rod and cone cells of the eye's retina. Rod cells (orange) and less numerous cone cells (blue) are specialized light-sensitive cells. They occur on the surface of the retina.

page 53: A cross section through a male human head that shows the brain and eyes in natural colors.

page 54: Artwork of a cross section through the ear, nose, and throat of a patient with excessive mucus production due to a cold.

page 57: A colored SEM micrograph of the tongue's touch-sensing cells.

page 58: Art showing the transmission of pain along the sensory nerves of the hand to the brain and back—in this case causing a person to move his hand away from a hot object.

page 61: Colored X-rays of healthy human hands at 3 years (left) and at 20 years (right). The child's hand has areas of cartilage in the joints between the finger bones (phalanges), where bone formation and growth will occur. Only a few of the eight wrist bones have formed. In the adult hand, all the bones are present and the joints have closed.

READ MORE ABOUT IT

Smithsonian Institution
www.si.edu

Center for Disease Control and Prevention
www.cdc.gov

U.S. Department of Agriculture's Nutrition home page
www.nutrition.gov

THE BRAIN
by Seymour Simon

THE HEART
by Seymour Simon

LUNGS
by Seymour Simon